SNOWY OWLS, EGRETS, & UNEXPECTED GRACES

"This is a book of magic spells, calling on birds, acts of art, blessings, and humble ritual to turn a time of illness to a quest for awareness. Small changes work the mysteries: not 'shadow of death' but 'death of shadow.' Not first-person predictable, but third-person intimate, a voice filled with surprises inhabiting daily life, life ritual, spoken scripture, 'the painful juxtaposition of various needs' converging polarities toward a hawk's whole vision, a thrush's solo song. The multiple realms of the awakened mind here (in titles like 'Sturgeon, Osprey, *Gemini New Moon*') give this writer and her readers a place to stand in a complex world, a place to understand, a place to heal, connect, be whole."
—KIM STAFFORD, author of *Wind on the Waves: Stories of the Oregon Coast*

"Gwendolyn Morgan has graced us with a new collection of poems that entreat us to lean into the world, into the vital conversation that awaits all who pay attention. She extends a thread of intimate observations through these poems, inviting us to remember the real world of nuthatches, chickadees, black-tail deer and mergansers. Woven into this vivid landscape, Gwendolyn extends her tender touch to the sorrows and suffering of modernity – cancer, capitalism, greed, violence, suicide – all seen through the heart of compassion and transmuted by the alchemy of her eloquence. We are awakened and healed through her generous offerings."
—FRANCIS WELLER, author of *The Wild Edge of Sorrow: Rituals of Renewal and the Sacred Work of Grief*

"Gwendolyn Morgan swept me away in the grace and the magnificence of her writing and her impassioned words. She evokes power and beauty into every aspect of nature and life – both the light and the shadow. *Snowy Owls, Egrets, and Unexpected Graces* is divinely inspired!"
—SANDRA INGERMAN, author of *Soul Retrieval* and *Walking in Light*

"How do I express the deftness with which Gwendolyn holds the reader – even the most broken of us – in a sacred web of healing? Her splendid sensitivity to the heart of the wild, and the heart of the wounded, come together in a volume of poetry that takes us back to the place where we are forever whole."
—JOAN BORYSENKO, author of *Minding the Body, Mending the Mind*

D1133781

"Gwendolyn talks to birds. They talk back.
The birds write. *Calligraphy tracks on the sand.*

Gwendolyn takes care of her people.
The fog settles into the chest cavities of those around us.

Gwendolyn reads the mystics. Cares for the sick.
Comforts the dying.

Spend some time with her.
She runs silent, runs deep."
—MICHAEL LERNER, author of *Choices in Healing*

Snowy Owls,
Egrets,
&
Unexpected Graces

GWENDOLYN MORGAN

HIRAETH PRESS
DANVERS, MASSACHUSETTS

Cover painting by Susan Bourdet, courtesy of Wild Wings
www.susanbourdet.com | www.wildwings.com

Cover and text design by Jason Kirkey

ISBN 978-0-9975927-0-2
First Edition 2016

Hiraeth Press books may be purchased for education, business or sale promotional use. For information, please write:

Special Markets
Hiraeth Press
P.O. Box 1442
Pawcatuck, CT 06379-1968

 HIRAETH PRESS

DANVERS, MASSACHUSETTS
www.hiraethpress.com

¶ Hiraeth Press is a publisher with a mission. We are passionate about poetry as a means of returning the human voice to the chorus of the wild.

with gratitude to the winged ones

CONTENTS

SUMMER SOLSTICE

Dearest Egret,

Each day you invite us
to remember
the scalloped shapes of
memories, shells,
dream fish, luminaries.

Thank you.

Corvidae, Summer Solstice

Corvus caurinus Northwestern crow. *khaaw! khaaw! khaaw!* How it is to talk to a young corvid that got temporarily stuck in the bardo of our shared backyard. Young Crow learning how to fly. Our neighbor holds young Crow upon her deerskin gloved hand, sees with Corvidae eyes, avian eyes. This is the turning of the wheel of the year, the landscape of crow mind: spiritual consolation, disconsolation. Luminous one, wisdom keeper, creator of the world. Familiar and conspicuous, beloved and despised. Crows. We listen to their distinct conversations. She says they have been guardians, sentinels at our house, guarding the four directions as well as *kairos* time – past, present, and future. Crow gazes intently into her eyes, her face. She makes clicking noises with her tongue, sings "Morning Sun," a Lakota Song, to this crow, softly. It is morning on the longest day of the year. Birds usually begin talking at daybreak, sometimes announcements or a series of mathematical equations we do not quite understand. Now I understand the warning *khaaws* at dawn: the distant neighbor's feral orange cat with the menacing face was bothering the little crow. I ran toward the cat "leave Crow alone!" and it hissed and spit at us with a malice I have not seen before, and lunged at me so I jumped back, grabbed the small metal trowels and banged them like cymbals until the cat left the yard. All the crows watched us. Then little crow resting upon her hand as she assisted it back to the Douglas fir, safely from murder in a murder of crows. Crow appears in our dreams, drawings, paintings, music and now in our common yard. *"One can do a lot worse than have the corvids as allies in the liminal space between the waking world & the unseen world!"*[1]

Yellow Cedar

Creating worlds, we choose one word over another: cherry blossom or plum blossom, eagle whistle or kestrel, stratus or nimbostratus, spells or incantations – seed syllables of the luminous auric field. She asks: *What emotion will you release so you may choose another?* Making choices involves constantly deciding what we want so we can let go of what does not suit us – the right line enjambment, an awareness, mindfulness, in breath, out breath. The raven laughs and her chortle is that raspy, yellow cedar bark sound of creation. Just as a seed contains the entire plant, the syllabic concentration of our intentions invokes kernels of seed corn, ley lines, filaments of light, illuminated text of psychic threads. *Pipsissewa,* pink wintergreen, pink florescence, moss-laden world of salal, elderberry, a holy syllabary. Our neighbor tells us we learned to weave from Grandmother Spider too. The first loom was of sky and earth chords, little hairgrass, red fescue, small flowered knotweed, lazy lines, horizontal bands, sunlight, white shell, lightning, indigo blue. *Tomorrow morning re-member yourself back. Thread your memories, hand-dyed. Stitch each piece together as the sun rises.*

Donkey Graces

"If a donkey brays in the morning,
Let the hay makers take a warning;
If the donkey brays late at night,
Let the hay makers take delight."[2]
—for Angelina

Plant three rows of organic heirloom carrots.
Buy a dozen pink ladies, apples from the orchardist down the lane.
Remember to have your hair styled, her hooves trimmed.

Massage the sway back of an older rescue donkey,
the thick charcoal gray stripe that runs vertical holds the myth that once upon a time
donkeys had unmarked gray fur, and that it was only after Christ's entry into Jerusalem
on the back of a donkey that they received the dark cross on their backs.

Watch the donkeys haul the peat like a wheelbarrow in an old Irish storybook,
 heal the ailing, the sorrowful, people and animals alike.

Remember Saint Nicolas used to wear the garment of a bishop
as he rode on the back of a donkey (no sleigh, no reindeer),
and in Egypt, donkey's milk was a cosmetic applied to ensure smooth skin.
Donkeys bring unfettered grace to each morning.

Take delight in the greeting bray of Angelina at dusk.
Buy a plush toy donkey named Esperanza.
Place dried red roses in her saddlebag, tuck one behind your ear.

Moon of Cherries Blackening

All full moons bring light to the dark, illuminating what we have left unattended in our unconscious, and what we need to see to move forward in our lives. The robins, cedar waxwing and scrub jays eat the cherries, reminding us of many dimensions of our capacity to envision a new global community. Continued unrest around the world, so whatever continent we turn to we witness political discord, inequality, habitat destruction, human rights violations, and yes, greed manifest in numerology in the marketplace. Stories from friends we know whose parents used to live in those countries remind us of our lost core values and of the power of love, community, connection. Our neighbor reminds us *Ansuz* is the messenger rune, the thirteen runes of the cycle of initiation, the rune of speech, songs, poems, incantations.[3] She is weeding, pulling pigweed out of the red chard. She reminds us that mid-summer we must take more time to be still, to meditate, contemplate, lie in the meadow grass, play our flutes, create art, sit by the river – whatever puts us in a quiet, receptive state, so we can grasp the special messages the Cosmos has for us, create peace in our souls to transform the world around us.

She Speaks for the Bees

> "...sweeter than honey,
> even the drippings from the honeycombs."
> —Psalm 19:10

Mama, what if there were no honeybees?
the six year old girl asks inquisitively,
auburn curls at her temples,
eyes the color of Hostas in late September.
She asks again her question about the bees.

I'm afraid it would be very sad.
The flowers and trees depend on them.
we all do.... Her voice trails off
as she considers how to explain the
complex process of pollination to a child.

Bees go from flower to flower, transforming nectar
into honey. They pollinate our favorite fruits
like Honeycrisp apples and Desiree peaches.
The girl sticks out her lower lip, the color of Pink Pearl apples,
pulls her teddy bear close to her chest. *It hurts when they sting us.*

Outside the hospital we watch the bees slowly
move from daisy to dahlia, the late-blooming flowers of autumn.
The mother with end-stage metastatic breast cancer
finding ways to tell her daughter that she was dying
now, along, with the bees.

In June we learned over 50,000 bees were found dead
outside the outlet mall in Wilsonville.
The flowering linden trees in the parking lot
sprayed with dinotefuran, a common insecticide,
clumps of dead bees on the sidewalks.

Monocrops replacing small diverse farms,
small selection of pollen, malnourished bees, neonicotinoids,
pharmaceuticals designed to mimic plant-based nicotine, climate change,
the long list of probable causes not unlike
the causes of cancer, no longer an epidemic; pandemic.

The bees with iridescent wings, delicate membranes, colonies,
queen bees with royal jelly, worker bees,
intricate communities, a part of the luminous thread,
sun-lit honeycombs dripping with ambrosia,
the music of thousands of wings.

The mother remembers playing Russian composer
Rimsky-Korsakov's "Flight of the Bumblebee" on her silver flute
as she watches the U.S. Security of State announce that Syria
"crossed global red lines."⁴ She closes her eyes
with the painful news clips, clumps of dead bodies on the sidewalks.

This afternoon she drinks tea with hibiscus, chamomile, peppermint
and rose petals, wishes she had enough breath to play her flute, winces.
Thousands of civilians in Damascus are found with neurotoxic symptoms.
How would anyone gas their people with sarin or any chemical weapon?
How would a military intervention not impact all the children of the world?

"Neither our country nor our conscience
can afford the cost of silence," the diplomat continues.
What about the destruction of the environment by our chemicals?
She asks questions while her daughter sleeps, wrapped in a soft floral blanket.
Do bees have a sense of righteous anger? About colony collapse?

Do they understand how sweet the laws of Nature?
Are they simply in deep grief as they hum another requiem?
She pauses. *I don't think the bees use expletives,* she says.
If they did – what would they tell us?

LAMMAS

italic handwriting as spiritual practice

birds write in italic
calligraphy tracks on the sand
bells, incantations, whistles,
imagine the *I Ching*, book of changes,
runes, hieroglyphics,
gallery-style psychic readings,
Gregorian chants
shamanic invocations
Gaelic prayers
geocentric aspects, ingresses, stations,
Om mani padme hūm, luminous bodies of birds
holy feathers, murmurations
linking us to the cosmos.

Mindfulness, Cortez Island

She walks along the edge of sky,
clouds, happiness
tells us today is a day to stop
to listen to the trees
tap into our inner wisdom.
We pick lavender, calendula, hollyhock.
She dabs the colors of the Salish Sea on
cold press watercolor paper
Paynes gray, cobalt blue, Prussian blue.
We pause, then continue with aimless wandering
among Canada geese, flowers, prayers,
afternoon kitchen preparatory mindfulness of
apricot, arugula, saffron rice
sea salt and lime,
graphic ephemeris of declination
on the Misty Isles.

In a time of crisis it is critical to note
we are connected with the plants.
Mullein is conspicuous for its
thick wooly leaves
tall stalks, small yellow flowers.
Like plant medicines, poems change consciousness
and trust contains *entheos*
light, phosphorescence.
We press flowers, wax-sealed, dream-like.
She says the words of the sky,
the flowers, and the little birds
speak to us
kinglet, wren, sparrow
interspecies telepathic communication,
animal wisdom, tree wisdom,
share your gifts, she says,
finish a sentence with bleed proof white,
the remembrance of their leaves, limbs, feathers.

Moon of Harvest

"*The voice of the dove is the rain song*,"[5] our neighbor reminds us. Mourning dove calls from the peaks of houses, misty rain just beginning at dawn, and continuing throughout the morning. "*Out of its mourning, the dove invokes new waters of life…reminds us that it does not matter what our life conditions, new waters and new life are possible.*"[6] We pick up stories, runes by moonlight: *Othala* and *Uruz*. *Uruz* is the energy of new forms emerging, strength, harvest, a change of consciousness, long curved horns of oxen, the frieze on the stone, the temple of Tarzien, drizzling rain. At the end of a long day, we learn one of our colleagues was killed in a Motor Vehicle Accident, MVA, while returning from fishing on the North Fork. The other driver intoxicated. Golden whiskey bottle on the seat, pale urine-colored beer in cheap aluminum cans in the cooler. We find a dead robin in the middle of the road, breast plumage bright pyrrol orange. This is a time of walking along other paths, *Othala* the rune of death and resurrection. Mourning doves call again back and forth. She says when an obstacle appears in our lives, it is the universe's way of redirecting us to grow even if it does seem unbearable at times.

Between memory and hope

"Listen to all the teachers in the woods. Watch the trees, the animals and all living things – you'll learn more from them than from books."[7]

Between memory and hope, imagination and logic, under nimbostratus clouds and presentiment of rain, we walk along the Salmon Creek trail listening to voices of crows, cottonwood trees, black-capped chickadees, belted kingfisher, water on river-stones. A rufous hummingbird appears in front of us, a female. I feel the flutter of wings, the northwestern wind in the leaves. I close my eyes and open them – she is hovering directly in front of my face, almost as in my dreams except in that numinous space the hummingbirds have spoken to me in a language I understand. Knowing the rain is coming may be that unexplainable evidence for an anomalous anticipatory effect in our autonomic nervous systems. Perhaps it is true that physiology changes in predictable ways in anticipation of and after exposure to emotional visual stimuli. Then the environmental exposure to toxins, which has led to this pandemic of auto immune disorders. She says she is taking a "media break," a sabbath from external soundings, the news or *not news* so depressing. We say our prayers of gratitude aloud, witnessed by marsh grasses, enormous blue dragonflies, white-breasted nuthatch, white-tailed deer, red fox, Pacific tree frogs. Between memory and hope, mists and birdsong, we remember the sky. *We listen to all the teachers in the woods.*

Moon of Brown Leaves

Drawing on the wisdom of our ancestors, the brown leaves, what our neighbor says the Lakota call *nagi*, "that which contains all the stories that have ever been told by me or about me or in my vicinity or by my ancestors."[8] White sage burns, smolders, smoke rises. The elder encircles us with the smoke of sage and prayers, blesses our hearts, our hands. We stand in a circle and walk clockwise around the circle. A red-tailed hawk lands in the Douglas fir above us, cries out, a *scree*. I remember the cardiac catheterization from earlier in the day: the long, thin, flexible tube she inserted into a blood vessel in his neck and threaded to his heart. The cardiologist placed a special dye in the catheter, which flowed through his bloodstream to his heart. We know the stories of this man having the procedure, years of relational pain, loss of love, series of losses, which flow through his life, and a build-up of resentments like the plaque hardening his coronary arteries. We see the runes: *Perth* sits at the heart of initiation and *Wunjoy*, "Joy," like a snake goddess carved into an oak tree. The old English word *glaed* meant joy and shining brightness. The sunlight streams through the brown leaves. The moon will rise in a few hours. A small rubber boa is curled beneath the pile of wood. The man came to the hospital alone. His skin is the color of the leaves, veined, damp.

AUTUMN
EQUINOX

Topaz Creek

All autumn
She walked along the paths
lined with blackberries, bachelor buttons
wild roses

each afternoon
the Welsh mountain ponies
with long manes and hope
would come running, shimmering
in expectation of apples
red and yellow pieces
mixed with rounds of orange carrots

each piece
held in the palm of her open hand

as she talked with them
she felt dreams
open like seed pods suddenly split
puffs and tassels blown
in the cobalt teal sky
like good omens for the future
filled with green gold leaves
the ache of sap slowing
with the trembling of the aspen

each season
the ponies grazed
in the pasture
the nutria carried long
green grasses in it teeth
across the small stretch
of Topaz Creek.

She listens closely to what the birds have to say

Red-throated loon speaks in Sanskrit.
Red-breasted merganser catches a small translucent white fish.
Two mergansers swim together in the salt water, one eating the fish.
To begin a poem she draws with a copper-colored pencil,
Swiss-made, like chocolate, yet almost the color of her skin,
the beach stones, the copper kettle her grandmother
brought back from Nova Scotia.
Gulls murmur on the beach, sitting on the sand,
wading in the shallow waters.
She was told pink was not a color to be worn or even liked
now it is the banner color for all breast cancer survivors,
certain fuchsia petals at the end of summer,
rose quartz, a healing heart stone.
She imagines a bird other than a flamingo wearing pink,
draws a circle for a mandala,
fills it with archetypal figures, dream animals, small birds,
constellations, hieroglyphics, sacred engraved writing of bird tracks.
She uses a white quill pen, a swan's flight feather,
honoring her ancestors who used quills for writing on parchment,
white on black, black on white.
The male common merganser has a green head and a red bill, the female
a wispy cinnamon crest. Both are usually silent, not pink, not out-spoken
offering a small croak or soft whistle when in flight.
She watches the loons, mergansers, grebes
swim and dive repeatedly as the day comes to a close.
The plovers, killdeer hurry along the mud flats making poignant comments.
In the woods, the Swainson's thrush is singing.
She listens closely to what the birds have to say.

Autumn Equinox

Kingfisher wears cerulean blue grey-white feathers
flies over the water with small even swoops.
She says she is beading the afternoon to evening

mindfully flying from thin tree branch to solemn stump
fishing for rainbow trout minnows, small water skippers.
Her iridescent fish scales are beaded to sun dogs,

atmospheric phenomena of cloud rainbows.
She loudly breaks the silence between the crows
with her announcement: *it is time!*

It is time to cradle the light of the afternoon sun.
It is time to have a small snack before dinner.
It is time to listen to the water on river-stones.

It is time to ease weary bones along deer trails
leading to pools of deep waters, past layers of fir and cedar,
leaves and mosses, layers of old intentions.

It is time to cultivate creativity, compassion,
silence, gentleness, peace.
It is time to welcome the balance

of light and dark, Libra New Moon,
round beads of galaxies,
star maps of our ancestors.

It is time to smooth feathers of fear and sadness,
to preen, to gather our dreams,
circles of women, poems,

heart beats on elk drum,
voices of flutes like bird song,
winged migrations, feathers,

repetitions of beads, voices, songs,
over and over. *It is time,*
she says, *it is time.*

Chokecherries

This year the sun turns to Libra later in the Gregorian calendar than usual, a balance of light and dark. Morning fog, chokecherries like prayer beads, warm afternoon sun. Rosehips round, red, full. Every morning the northwestern crows circle over my head when I pass a certain Douglas fir tree or the enormous western red cedar. They fly in a circle or an oval overhead, quietly, morning and evening. I wonder if these are the same sentinels that often appear to guard the four directions of our home. I have ridden my bicycle over 10,000 miles, back and forth to work, a short commute in seven years. How many years have the crows been watching, circling, protecting? Perhaps we are only asleep as Hafiz, Rumi and the esoteric traditions of mystics would suggest. We feed crows last week's challah this day before Sabbath eve. Crow takes one large piece and flies to share it with companions. The cedar waxwings are plentiful this year, and alternate with the crows along with all the smaller songbirds and passerines visiting us. Black-capped chickadee. American goldfinch. English sparrow. House finch. Spotted towhee. Our neighbor tells me that she has felt weary, tired again. She minimizes her fatigue, says perhaps it is the ache of autumn, anticipation of rain. We walk along the edge of the afternoon, listening to the sky. Her stories gleaned here when we feed the songbirds, gathering red millet, sunflower seeds, warmth, water, syllabic resonance, a worldview that recreates our experience of reality. We walk along the path believing in bone structure, form, length of tail, wingspan.

Kestrel, watching

The Ana's hummingbird chases the belted kingfisher in circles over Turtle Pond, repeated again and again. Both of these birds make vocalizations we have not heard before except from ground squirrel alarms while near the Breitenbush River, hours away. Iridescent red crown, gray-edged feathers slate blue above a musical trill. We feel dusted with bleary, hopeful, and bleak news from here and afar and wish it were yellow late-blooming chrysanthemum pollen and rainbow trout scales. Fairy dust. Occupy Portland, Seattle, Vancouver, Wall Street, New York City, London, Arab Spring. Protests in Chile, Nigeria, Burma, Syria, Turkey. Ferguson. Rallies once were held in over a thousand cities in Europe, Africa, Asia, South and North America. Last Spring twenty-nine civilians died in Tunisia near the Tunis Bardo Museum. This summer 49 sisters and brothers in Orlando, countless in Baghdad. We count continents, epidemics, coups d'état. Nations chase one another in the global roundabout of economics, creature comforts, religious conflicts and territorial dives. Our goal is to not drink coffee or cocoa, avoid bananas, mangoes, and purchase locally, and we slip back to fair trade and local companies. Northwestern coffee and tea snobs. A young man jumped off the Interstate Bridge into the Columbia River in despair on Thursday. Every day we have people of all ages, genders, religious preferences, sexual orientations, body types, personality types, spiritual paths, haircuts, arrive at the hospital with SI = Suicidal Ideation. A small kestrel sits in the tree over the meadow, watching.

Deer has Full Tail
New Moon

In a time beyond memory: look for calligraphy pens and nibs. Relearn to write your ancestors' alphabet, runes. Wind and weather spirits, birds, native ornithology. Stillness and silence, migratory. How we walk between shadows, outstretch our feathers and wings. What it is that makes a place, a day, a moment. The ineffable presence of divinity. Animate, invest, enliven. The doe and her two fawns stand beside the dry Queen Anne's lace on Salmon Creek Avenue. "Good Morning!" I greet them as I pass by on my bicycle. Thousands of people march in the city blocks of thirteen cities around the country for what might be called "Occupy Peace." Standing up, walking through the dry stalks of our economies on the deer-skinned fringes of our streets for social justice, peacemaking, hope, courage, common sense. Our neighbor says we might have protested sooner, louder, longer. She says she has begun to play her mother drum in the morning. She is sitting on the earth for a few minutes each day to recalibrate. Columbia white-tailed deer return from a distant time.

Moon of Falling Leaves

Mhende designs. Henna veins of leaves, repeated patterns of our lives. She invites us to paint with espresso, the thick dregs at the bottom of the cup, or what is left in the round crystal wine goblet, the cabernet sauvignon from an aged bottle of fine French wine. Remnants. We create patterns with wine corks with rubber bands around them. Grasses, borders appear. She says she hasn't had a drink for centuries, reminds us not to use too many colors from our palette on one illustrated journal page. We create "spirit drawings"[9] and we see lines remembering the essence of corn stalks, rosemary twigs, vine maple leaves, a sculpted copper horse. The snippets of color, bits of things are like her dream fragments. Sky windows, small picture window boxes with weather poetics. I draw a crow, bird tracks. Song birds emerge from the maple leaves. She says the strokes and tones may speak their own language. I pick up a rune by moonlight: *Naudhiz*, the rune of *need-fire*, a fire kindled at times of hardship.[10] We gather leaves the color of gingerbread, press them in the back of an old field guide to birds that no longer has a cover or title page. Each form, each feather, each leaf, each vein has a story. Today, falling leaves are our teachers.

SAMHAIN

Til kær

She wakes early
in midst of translucent dreams
Great Horned Owl
calls from the Douglas fir
Coyote from the meadow
below the old barn
where the Percheron
and assorted draft horses used to rest.
Now black-tailed deer glean
the last of the roses, apples,
greens from the garden.
With gratitude, she greets them,
remembers the Danish of her ancestors,
Til kær, "to hold dear."
Oh, to be love!

The rabbits orient themselves
toward the carrots
she scatters for them
orange pieces of root vegetables
near the mossy green bird bath.
The rabbits and the deer remind her
that we are an open book
a chapter of soul
seen by the winged ones, the birds
and the animals
who journey with us
in dream time, in waking.
She imagines their field notes
of awareness of our passages.

The Language of Birds, Scorpio New Moon

Congas, low whistle, gourd, bass guitar, Native American flute in the key of G. She said to look for your soul in the long lines of dreams, a flute underneath your voice, slim veil of crescent moon, shadows within shadows. Light unto light, look through the darkness, the jasmine flowers unbelievably still blooming, sweet potato pie, watercolor blocks, the increase in volume, healing. The language of birds is a symbolic one. "We have been taught the language of birds (*'ullimna mantiq at-tayr*) and all favours have been showered upon us."[11] When you listen, you will go far on your journey, even when the sky is clouded and still, a thin pencil line of geese in the distance. She says each of us brings our shadow, the reflection of our own self, forgiveness, remembrance; sepia blends with deep green to sienna like the sound of your voice, the lyrics of your family tree. Let dreams hold the shuffle of hammer dulcimer, clarinet backing vocals. One song gives you more light, and hope melts inside us as saffron beads soften in basmati rice.

Moon of Starting Winter

Sterling jay announces the gray squirrel. Frost on the ground. Seventeen titmice eating suet. In the gallery, the raven's eye has a small round fragment, piece of crystal, granite or something else that is shiny, that catches the light. Field notes about bird nests: pendulous, cavity, platform and cusp nests. And the raven brings light, returns the sun, pecking at her classroom window in Neskowin, pounding on the door, startling her. Not a ghost or a silent scavenger in the playground, yet a song, a throaty *tok! tok!*, an incantation, an invitation into dreamscape with black feathers, silver-black beak, archival, numinous, flying with wing feathers engraved like topographical maps from another century, flying over a small stone oven with round loaves of bread, kernels of wheat, candle flames, red-shafted flickers of songs, perceptions, references to wars repeated. Repeated again, here, now. Another death of a child soldier on another continent, repeated again and again. Over twenty percent of our children are living in food insecure households, go to bed hungry in a country of abundance. Famine continues for decades in sub-Saharan Africa. Now Ebola. Here, a local epidemic of pertussis. Luminous maple leaves, Oregon white oak leaves, acorns, hazelnuts. The raven picks a hazelnut up in her beak and flies west, away, reflection in the autumn window, in the direction of ocean, veins of water like ley lines, topographical maps, blind contour drawings.

Egrets, Lymph Nodes, Solar Eclipse

The language of birds is symbolic language, angelic language, rhythmic language. This language – like the landscape – shapes the song of the soul. She spoke of the alchemical art of the ten *paramitas*, the breath of the spotted owl. *Samavritti* signifies equal or same turning. Breathing in and out, allow each inhale and exhale to be equal in length and quality, duration and quality. Cold and wetness, in-breath and out-breath. Be surprised by nothing. Great egret, rising white from the creek at daybreak. Rain returns from the north, then snow. White upon white. She reminds us to listen to what others may name as ordinary or common birds, who speak the language of the divine too. That the solar eclipse reminds us of our connection to the Galactic Center. She spoke of a pain in her lymph nodes, said she must be fighting off an infection, was drinking more *mate*, green tea, water. Her diet she tended as carefully as the birds. We watched again as Canada geese flew overhead, so close we felt the warmth of their bodies, heard the beat of each wing, migratory, our longing for that greater sense of belonging, the return to a remembered dream. She said the soft brown of their belly feathers was the color of my tea, tea so thick with milk and honey the morning tasted like the promised land. The celestials sounded a celebratory note like the geese honking, inviting us to fly south for a few months, even a night, join the heartfelt V-formation. Long undulating lines called us back to the present moment, our breath, the muted blue-gray autumn sky, the lines of geese, cirrostratus clouds, snow melt, tealight, sun on fir and pine needles – the images of returning.

Owl Meadow, Lunar Eclipse no. 2

"Listen to the howl of our spiritual
brother, the wolf, for how it goes with
him, so it goes for the natural world."[12]

At four o'clockish in the morning there is an in-breath, sharp, frosty. We hear a voice
in the dark, "It's time to get up." A slip of the shadow of Earth over the moon, loss
of light, interruption of transmissions of electromagnetic energy. We walk under
the starry sky, watching, listening. Coyote in Owl Meadow, a sharp bark, dog-like.
Our dogs on high alert, ears erect. Fog rising from the Salmon Creek tributary, from
the north. A man in Washougal set his home on fire, shot his dogs, his Significant
Other, someone else. The front page photo shows workers sifting through ashes,
bone fragments.[13] White supremacist, anti-government. White man. Had he been a
man of color it would have been headlines around the world: terrorist in our midst.
His house with more armaments than the local National Guard armory and the
nearest Army base combined. Crazy Uncle. Ten more wolves shot in Idaho, Montana,
Wyoming. Fragmentation of Rain Forest. Fracking in the High Plains. She says the
Sabian symbols for this Full Moon urge us to learn from the past and envision a
better future.[14] More darkness over the moon as we walk quietly through the early
morning, Douglas fir, western hemlock frosted with ice, silhouettes of wisdom.
Coyote pack yipping in the distance.

Moon of Shedding Horns

It was snowing when I saw the doe with the hurt leg standing in the winter wheat grass near the side of the road. I was peddling my bicycle north, and tiny flakes of snow were coming down. This is near the place where we found the long-tailed weasel, not far from where we saw the 3-pronged buck in autumn months. I stopped my bike, spoke to her softly, imagined the twin fawns and yearling that often accompany her waiting behind the apple trees. Black-tailed deer. She watched, listened, flicked her ears. Once in the snowy hills we found a small set of antlers on a tiny skull base. Aurora borealis overhead. *Kenaz* signifies "torch" and is the rune of opening, clarity, fire, lightbearing. Hestia's fire is the fire of the hearth, the center of the world, the gate of life and death. A friend texts to say they saw snowy owls on the northern coast near Orcas Island, then another snowy owl near Eugene, a long flight from their Arctic homeland. The dogwoods, crab apples are bare, whereas the northern bayberry and staghorn sumac have berries and clusters of red fruit throughout these gray months. The flag was at half-staff, lowered in honor of another young man killed in active duty in Afghanistan. He was the son of the woman who saved an injured bald eagle a few years back. *"Was this an omen, then?"* she asks at the funeral chapel. We hear the melody to *Silent Night* played on an upright mahogany piano. The doe turns and ambles down toward the creek. A spotted towhee hops in front of her, and they both slip out of view

WINTER
SOLSTICE

Snowy Owls and Unexpected Graces

How they come, unexpected
almost as if visitors
from another realm
transcendent, magical
white plumes of snow
flight feathers.

When we are in balance
our *chi* flows
through our bodies
with no blockage,
the body is well.
When there is a blockage
of that energy,
problems develop.
Our bodies mirror the earth.
This winter the owls fly south
in migrations, irruptions.

The owls are a catalyst
of remembering that
we all know who we are,
of how to be a spirit,
to be seen for who we are
round yellow eyes, gilded
wisdom of the movements
of common voles, field mice,
wind, weather patterns.
They wing their way through time,
appearing in Paleolithic
cave art in Ariege, France,
this morning near the airport.

Grace is the flight of the owl, silent
as the synapses of neurons
regeneration of tissue,
synergistic healing,
skimming over the frozen earth
ice-crystals, wisdom, silence
illuminated.[15]

Trumpeter Swans, Winter Solstice

Weeks of fog enshrouding the trees, the land, low to the ground early in the morning, rising slowly, sometimes breaking through to sunlight. Thirty miles away the mountains sparkle with the last sun and moon square of this turning of the wheel of the year. Dusky geese and snow geese overhead. Two trumpeter swans, a snowy egret and a blue heron together on the mud flats along Salmon Creek. Geocentric aspects, ingresses of snow. Two days of rain betwixt and between. The temperature fluctuates between twenty-one and forty-six degrees Fahrenheit. We avoid stores, catalogs, newspapers, internet advertisements, go back and forth between work and venture out beyond our daily trap-lines to buy two weeks' worth of groceries. A high-grade consumptive fever settles in like the fog. Greed and Retail, for 'tis the season to present what is "needed" for happiness. The fog settles in to the chest cavities of those around us: bronchitis, pneumonia. Our neighbor is homebound for a week with an upper respiratory infection, and she says she can't get out to feed her birds; we bring her mail, vegetable soup, feed the birds. The neighbor who owns the llamas down the road dies of middle-class pneumonia after the couple lost their jobs and their health benefits and he waited too long to go the hospital emergency room. "Tragedy…" the hospital pulmonologist, ICU intensivist and internal medicine physicians all repeat. Our country as the global tragedy, a low-grade theatre production on how to fail in health care, social services and education. Garnering hope, we read the mystics and metaphysicians of old, stories, legends, have friends over for dinner or tea, listen to songs, write music in our dreams. The sparrows gather in the heart space of our communities. We feed them commercial bird seed, knowing better given all the arguments for changing migration patterns by the provision of food sources in unlikely places, yet the gathering of twenty songbirds in the yard brings joy. The northern flicker, western gray squirrel and series of three jays – western scrub, Stellar's and blue jay scare the little birds away. Winter wren, black-capped chickadee, Oregon juncoe, bushtit. The last day of the sun in Sagittarius. The light will begin to return tomorrow.

Gathering, Capricorn New Moon

Incandescent skein of fog along the creek. Late morning, bird count. Tundra and trumpeter swans, dusky geese, great blue heron, common egret, a pair of bald eagles, spotted towhee, ruby-crowned kinglet, bushtit, black-capped chickadee, myriads of ducks – goldeneyes, pintails, wood ducks, buffleheads, hooded mergansers, wigeons. Winter wild grasses with seeds. The magical scientific leap into conscious unconsciousness. How the northern flicker eats the suet. The gray squirrel carries the *mazorcas*, dry ear corn cobs, along the cedar fence, up into the curly willow – an enormous leap into the Douglas fir. Gathering: how she turns a word, a series of words into a poem, doesn't take a nap. Keeps collecting phrases. Raccoon tracks in the backyard. The alchemy of the last line. She tells us she has felt weary yet well enough to drum in the morning. We hear drumming in the distance: skin drum. Djembe, bodhran. Medicine drum. Hundreds of years ago, this morning repeats itself in the heart beat of the moose hide.

She Talks to the Sparrows

We wander under the blue-ing sky, now violet-blue, altostratus clouds on the edges of the horizon. Evening falls quickly. An ambulance, white and red, in front of our neighbor's house. It takes a half an hour to stabilize her in the gurney in the back of the vehicle. Crow in the Douglas Fir tree behind, black and green. She said the little people woke her, told her to get up. That she has field mice under her house. They take the bird seed from her feeder and carry it in the dryer vent. Who would put a vent near the ground? New construction – quick, fast money, poor quality – this house, unlike the white farm house with black trim at the end of the street – won't be here in a century. Her shoulder muscles are contracted, tight, like crooked willow limbs, like our global vision contracted by the economy of our myopic vision of future for the next seven generations. Even the masseuse cannot get the knots out, release months, years, decades of holding tightly. She says each day opens new ornithological fractals. The song sparrows sing, tan and brown. She talks to each one. The wind picks up, tosses the wind chimes, Key of A flat. "Spirits," she says quietly. She says every hair on our head is counted, every sparrow. She can't find one of her sable paintbrushes. She saw someone move the blinds. She heard noises in the kitchen. Not the field mice.

Butternut Squash Soup

Today I tell her I will write a poem about butternut squash soup
with winter pears, ginger, garlic, carrots, pepper
the woman who was assaulted, how she wept
holding the stuffed giraffe, honey stick and prayer shawl
the week of incessant rain, global warming,
how the dead bees rained on her sun porch,
how she crawled under the car to get out of the rain
when he left her bloody and bruised at the county park
how the soup is blended, smooth, a rusty orange-brown
like the round edges of screws on the Forest Service green picnic tables,
the edges of his silver truck bed. How she wears amber, a round
gemstone from the Dominican Republic, warm light of hope.
How Aglaia, Euphrosyne and Thalia dispense charm and beauty.
How bees pollinate the squash, pears, vegetables, herbs and spices.
How the honeycombs are lit from within, pure chroma color.
Hexagonal, esoteric shape of bees' bodies.
How the brush rabbit hopped quietly by, looking at her, worried.
This poem is about equilibrium in the midst of social media,
how another acquaintance spiraled out, anxiety, depression,
perhaps multiple personalities, or personality disorder
which doesn't exist in the latest DSM-5. What would his
diagnosis be anyway? Charismatic sociopath? He is
the neighbor next door who mows your grass, removes wasp nests,
when you haven't asked, and fixes the elderly neighbor's fence, her fence,
and how you would never suspect he was a predator
or that he might fly a jet plane with passengers aboard into the mountain
unless you were paying attention, watching the bees and stirring the soup
with a wooden spoon, adding a bit of Mediterranean sea salt.

Moon of Hard Times

Yet another powerful solar flare occurred, a coronal mass ejection generating geomagnetic storms, which affect everyone on this planet Earth. Our cell phones do not work and we do not receive emails for a time. The chestnut-backed chickadee has returned for a short visit, stopping by between the time of the ground frozen and the cherry blossoms. She spoke of exquisite bird cages carved with flowers and *animalitos* she had seen in Oaxaca, Otavalo, Cuenca, and again spirit houses of teak and bamboo in Sikhiu, Naypyidaw (formerly Rangoon). The rune *Berkano* is one of the birch tree, growth, seasonal rebirth. She told me she never imagined having a *mucinous* tumor in her belly – fourteen centimeters, probably benign, yet enormous and surrounded by fluid. We will care for her house while she is away, plan meals, visits to the hospital. Everything swollen – her abdomen, inflation, the pussy willows, words of the clinical staff, the flowering daphne, the moon.

Crows Talking, Lunar New Year, Aquarius New Moon

"The image for Aquarius, the Water Bearer, symbolizes a pouring forth of universal ideas and the baptism of humankind into collective consciousness,"[16] Surgery on the New Moon, five pounds of fluid for Aquarius. She was so tiny, where was the cyst? It was the size and shape of the egg she found on Vashon Island a summer ago. She had had dreams of eggs, quail-sized eggs, gemstones, healing necklaces, rituals. While she was in Peru the elder *ayahuascero* from the Amazon basin had blown something out of her belly space. She felt it go. She said post-op abdominal gas is more painful than running the San Francisco marathon, a race she ran over thirty years ago. In refugee camps around the world the food has been in short supply, the water rationed; they have not been able to do simple surgeries in years. She said there were crows outside her hospital window, sitting on the chapel steeple, talking.

IMBOLC

An urgent message from ruby-crowned kinglet

Faith of olive-green wings
a small red circle on her crown,
kwee! kwee! kwee!
an insistent call and tapping
at her studio window as
the kinglet flies from the western red cedar
back and forth from the tree to her window.

Once, in winter, she found a kinglet hopping up and down
retrieving droplets of moisture perhaps
or tiny insects from the sword fern
as if the little bird knew this is one of the places
outside the woods where there are no
insecticides.

This afternoon the kinglet returns
as the squirrels run up and down the cedar,
round eyes warm and bright
looking right at her, attentive,
even when she moves slowly toward the window
and back to the desk, with post-op fatigue.

Why do they come to us, the birds, the animals?
What is their need for acknowledging our waking?

Moon of Popping Trees

Spirals of birds on migratory routes. Thousands of songbirds in a vortex, a whorl, spinning through the sky, black on gray murmurations mid-winter. She said to hold a question in mind, walk in nature, expect that the uni-verse will provide you with guidance in the form of an omen. One song, many voices of birds. Unidentifiable. She said it was not benign after all. She said she never imagined that western medicine would be so disconnected from the soul. Years of psychological, spiritual, clinical research indicating the value of holistic therapeutic interventions – narrative psychiatry, storytelling, art therapy, music therapy, pet therapy, positive imaging, meditation, bodywork, acupuncture, the integrative list is voluminous. *Ehwaz* signifies "two horses" and is a rune of transit, transition, transformation. She said she felt she was the old mare put out to pasture, not Rhiannon the Mare Goddess, as no one in the clinic even asked her about herself. What was sacred, what brought meaning and purpose, let alone spiritual practices. They just asked if she wanted – no, told her that the social worker would be calling her (implied concern). *The cherry trees are budding*, she said. Then, *the varied thrush is back*. Raised eyebrows, oh, that is *nice*. She tried to tell the clinical staff about the flight plans of birds – who winging at speeds up to forty miles per hour, an entire flock of thousands of birds can make hairpin turns in a heartbeat. They said her blood pressure was low, perhaps bird watching was helpful. Acoustic, visual group soul of ten thousand wings.

The seventeenth day after she began chemotherapy, Pisces New Moon

The rains continue, heavy, insouciant sheets of rain. Spotted towhee watches the gray squirrel bury kernels of corn in the lawn. She said her friend went riding her bicycle, and stopped to sit by the lake. A storm blew in, and the wind whipped up – it blew all the hair from her head. That was the seventeenth day after she began chemotherapy. Another friend had a tribal elder cut her fifteen inch braid off, like women do when a loved one has died. Another just went in for a crew cut and the hair dresser asked if she was joining the Army, and she said "Yes, the breast cancer brigade." She said she had entered the cancer industrial complex. Even Angelina Jolie had a bilateral mastectomy and partial hysterectomy. She said the sun's exact conjunction with Chiron invites us to resolve long-standing issues. The puddles of rain water gather. Mallards fly overhead, turn, land in the water. Teal and brilliant blue on their wings. She says all healing involves acceptance and gratitude for even the most painful times and teachers.

Moon of Bright Snow

Five bald eagles fishing in the creek, circling the marsh each afternoon at the same time, whistling and calling back and forth. She began chemotherapy nearly a month ago. The Full Moon rises above the barren ash trees. Even here there were rumors of hail, snow. *Hagalaz* is the rune of disruption. A coyote pack making their rounds through the wild roses, oak, and alder trees. She said it was difficult to make sense of their tracks in the morning, round and round the trees, through the creek and across Owl Meadow, tracking mud on the fleece of snow. Their tracks reminded her of C. G. Jung's conversations about a *numinosum*. She said it is the sacred, luminous, inexplicable premonition of what might be experienced in the world, each breath. The sound of the wings of twenty-three bush tit on a square of suet, the birds then flitting off to the small trees to eat tiny insects. The coyote tracks. The eagles. Each breath. The rescue of a young man living with developmental delays by a stranger – he had walked ten miles to the river from his group home, and decided to swim in the river in which he would have drowned.[17] The Coors Light beer can she finds beneath the great horned owl's nest. She imagined the owl shaking its head in disbelief as the spirits of the wind blow through the branches

Mercury Retrograde, chemotherapy

A steady week of rain. The pair of bald eagles and red-tailed hawk circle Owl Meadow when the weather is fair. Whistles, high cries in the distance, rain. The Pacific tree frogs have begun their pre-spring chorus, repeating and repeating songs through the night. Flocks of birds returning, a hundred cedar waxwings, a half dozen ospreys, more random sightings of snowy owls. She tells me about avian migration and most specifically *migratory connectivity*, the six wing spans of separation, linking individual birds and persons throughout the wheel of the year. She says the chemotherapy is the worst thing she can remember experiencing. She remembers drumming all night for a healing. She remembers banding birds in the summer with little metal tags. These days birds carry transmitters, highly sophisticated GPS that allow the observer to track them anywhere in the world via satellite. Telemetry, like in the cardiac units of medical centers, except for the birds. She tells me that avian interior connectivity is far more sophisticated than miniaturized geolocators, or any of our electronics. Mercury retrograde, along with a number of large solar flares, offers to distort wireless communication. If only we would listen to our feathered sisters and brothers.

SPRING
EQUINOX

Red-shouldered Hawk, Healing Circles

Red-shouldered hawk
circles overhead, over the meadow, Topaz Creek
She says, *whatever your need for healing,*
the world has need too
the polar caps, glaciers, melting
earthquake, volcano, tsunami
pandemic of cancer, auto immune disorders.
She remembers to breathe
in a culture of non-breathing.
We are holding our breath.
The spotted owl waits
on the edge of the mixed riparian forest.
Write all this down in your dreams, slowly.
This buteo is very vocal, with distinctive, far-carrying calls.
This wood owl with strong resonant hooting,
white marks on scapulars.
Is there something in your life
you want to heal?

Robins, Runes, Osprey

"Take the breath of the new dawn and make it part of you.
It will give you strength."[18]

We walk along in the dark listening to the robins singing up the sun into the sky. Snow, hail, rain, sun, the weather a blend of winter, early spring. The moon intensifies gravitational pulls on tectonic plates, tidal flows, and our psyches as well. The robins have a unique happiness song, a repetition of *cheerio* that they sing at dawn during this time of year. Gradually the other birds join in, a comforting chorus. The osprey finally returned to Salmon Creek this week, six osprey at once circling us over the creek, chirping, whistling, calling, diving for fish. We watch them plunge into water with their feet first using a reversible front talon and food pads with tiny spicules for grasping slippery trout and salmon. They impale the fish upon a broken off branch and filet it slowly, seeming to enjoy the process of eating too. Occasionally they return as early as February, and this spring we asked: how do they know that this year is particularly cold and wet, and to wait until April to return from Mazatlan, Puerto Vallarta, even Tegucigalpa and San Salvador? *Raidho* follows the path of the sun, the wheel of the seasons, the round of life and is a rune of journey, communication, reunion. Today our neighbor tells us she is nauseous, and politely declines our offer of clam chowder. The chemotherapy is cumulative, she reminds us, and this round appears to be taking a toll. She says clinical journeys are private, painful, often lived alone without enough support in our isolated culture. She has a circle of friends and former colleagues who bring soup, crackers, visits, bird song applications on their *iPods,* a medley of needed things. Too many others receive unsolicited advice, the recommendations and judgments of those who are scared of the "C" word, worried for their loved ones. She reminds us that we, like the robins, are harbingers of hope too.

Moon Fattening

Full Moons bring light to the dark, illuminating what we need to see and change. Yesterday she shared that just as she was completing her chemotherapy treatment, a young woman was quietly ushered into a private room, accompanied by her significant other and her parents. She noted this woman had no aura – her pale skin ghostly, her slight figure barely visible – she appeared to be near death's door. Her mother took a quick phone call outside the room, *"she looks really bad…"* hushed, strained tones. In previous treatment days she had found this young woman's presence irritating because she was prone to non-stop talking quite loudly about herself, the 40 pounds of fluid in her belly, her previous active life. Now she wandered in her heart, felt sadness that she had less compassion and patience for this young woman's need to talk – perhaps this girl knew she was nearing the end of her life and it was all stumbling out: how she wanted to go backpacking like she did last summer, her need for assistance to do anything now, all of her dreams of her young life like candy wrappers strewn around her bed. Her Portuguese water dog whining in consolation. The scrub jays raucous and unrelenting in their vexation with a western gray squirrel. It was, she realized, the painful juxtaposition of our various needs, interconnected, intertwined and sometimes at odds with one another: silence and privacy, talking and connection, deep listening. *Thurisaz* is the divine portal between the celestial and the mundane, a giant rune of breaking down boundaries. She said that three planets changed direction within a couple of days of this Full Moon, emphasizing the need to shift how we see, feel and respond to the world.

Desire no. 2, Taurus New Moon

Desire. She says it takes time to listen to spring, walk among the trillium, lamb's tongue in the woods, large red tulips in the garden. To eat oatmeal for breakfast, drink brown rice tea, honeyed amber-light of early sun. How to celebrate being in a body on this earth when living with chronic illness? How to tell the neighbors not to use round-up, insecticides, pesticides that she felt were a link to cancer. How to remember connections, honor relationships? Then the rain, weariness and sadness; very heavy, a weight of vernal equinox weeks past – what is not yet, though the hyacinth, violets, cherry blossoms swath the air with moist scent as longing sometimes does. The desire to be unrestrained, to show up, even dance *salsa* or *merengue*. The fluidity of limbs, music, blood shimmering as the petals of these enormous tulips in the unexpected birth of light, death of shadow.

BELTANE

Diurnal Raptors

What do the birds of prey have to tell you?
Pause, she says, feel the wind in your tail feathers
Red-tailed Hawk carries your prayers
from earth to heaven,
like Golden Eagle, holding a higher perspective
numinous in the sheen of rain, sun-lit.

Look carefully at the letter shapes
of your life,
your intentions
the vowels and consonants
accipiters, buteos, falcons, harriers.
Prayers of intercessions
have similar postures.

Write on damp clay tablets
so mistakes may be
easily smoothed out,
conversations and requests noted
like little white field mice
scurrying underneath
the winter wheat.

Kestrel comes from another
direction, a diagonal line.
landing on a Douglas fir limb
which slopes to the earth
as an incantation.
Wing your way through
the sorrow,
lift your wings in gratitude.

Moon of Planting

The cedar waxwings are back, flocks of hundreds again this year. She tells me she follows the natural rhythm of her energy, though does not feel very good physically, therefore her emotions tip southward. She repeats words like bruised, fatigued, symptomatic, photosensitive, the cancer industrial complex. She is more animated about violet-green swallows, pink columbine, rain, water-soluble color pencils, acrylic paints. In the midst of remembering vulnerability, she is drumming, painting, beading again. Friends bring more gifts: fetish, amulet, bead, story, poem, incense, paintbrush, turquoise. She has swabs of dull pain. The rash on her face is visible and she pulls up her old cotton jeans to show me two red, sore and swollen spots on her legs, one on her right shin and one just below her left knee. Worrisome. She speaks of her efforts not to perseverate: spider bite? pulmonary embolism? reaction to some essential oil? stress? photosensitivity? food allergy? symptom from reaction to taxol, neulasta, carboplatin or something else? She speaks of listening to our elders. She speaks about the importance of *being* peace and *being* love – and to embody this way of being twenty-four hours a day. "When your body and mind are not one, you do not see deeply," she says. "But mindfulness brings you there, to the present, and then you see. Train yourself all day long to bring your mind to your body and to be present with your food, your friends, your work, everything, because the more you concentrate, the deeper you will see."[19] Early evening, the Moon floats above the horizon.

Sturgeon, Osprey, *Gemini New Moon*

She said it was a clear, hot day and the water was high after all the rain. Belted kingfisher and an osprey fishing. She was nauseous from the chemotherapy, yet thought it would be healing to be out along the river since she only had a few weeks left of treatment. She was in a dense medication fog with mild cognitive impairment, thinking in short sentences. She saw a couple walking on the tracks on the south side of the Lewis River Bridge, and realized it was the young woman from Waianae. Then she heard the train. The Amtrak train traveling south from Seattle hit the girl. She had maybe half a minute to clear the bridge, get off the tracks, yet stood there like deer in the headlights, frozen. Our neighbor said it was as surreal as the fusion clinic when someone in the next chair is told they have a few weeks to live, yet have time to say goodbye. The breath stops then. The young woman loved to camp and fish, and her boyfriend said she had caught her first sturgeon a month prior. Officials commenting on her death stated that someone is killed by trains on Washington state tracks every month.[20] New moons mark the ending of one lunar cycle and an opportunity to spiral to another level of learning. The osprey circled, chirping, joined by another and then another, a trio circling above.

Color Wheel no. 2, Moon of Good Berries

"Listen to the animals and they will teach you
the birds of the air and they will tell you. . . ."[21]

She says that now is the time to put together what we have learned so far.
Complementary colors, emotions, analogous spiritual practices,
pranayama techniques, breathwork, drum beats, blessings. If you change one of your
primary thoughts, what happens? How does that affect the moment? Paint a robin in
your journal and a robin is waiting on your front lawn every time you open the door.
Perylene red and cadmium yellow feathers, blended to look like mandarin oranges.
The grass is phthalo blue, and cadmium yellow, sap green, shadow green. The transit
of Venus allows us to follow the optical changes that take place during a transit. *Dagaz*
is a rune of transformation signifying "the light of day."

The house finch have returned following the robins. She says our life on earth is so
tenuous and fragile, impermanent and precious. She paints the common yellow-
throat yellow, brown, white; mixes the colors to have a warm rich earth color, then
black. Riverine floodplain habitat, semi-permanent wetlands, cottonwood-dominated
riparian corridors, remnant stands of white oak, fields of raspberries, strawberries,
blackcaps. No more chemotherapy, no radiation. She said the doctors gave her a
clean slate. Another woman who began treatment with her was placed on hospice.
The crow tracks in the sand look like a new series of runes.

Walking in the morning, we heard a sparrow repeating the same two notes like "spar-
row" and she identified the notes as C-A, like the beginning of the folk song "this
old man" repeated again and again. No cancer (CA) for now. This morning another
sparrow sings, repeated three notes, two the same one, up a note. She says to listen
closely and take the time to be clear, to allow conversation to be a practice of spiritual
presence. What about the crows? Allow each activity to be one of mindfulness. Be
like a slaty-breasted tinamou or a song sparrow who brings joy and grace into every
moment.

Yes, the crows are rebuilding their nest behind our houses. She wants a hermit thrush
to land on the verdant meadow grass and sing together with the song sparrow and
marsh wren. Surely you will allow the winged ones to teach you?

Corvidae Gratitude

Dear Raven,
This morning, the day after Summer Solstice
you called *tok tok tok*
as you flew overhead in greeting
black archival wings glossy with violet
bluish-greenish wing coverlets
abstract bristles at your beak.
I want to tell you *thank you*
with my own long and pointed wings
gather the wild foxglove,
long flowering, heart-healing bells
"foxes' music" they were called,
build a nest of sticks interlaced with poetics.
I want to say *thank you*
as I place a raven's feather
on the altar
remember you brought light to the Tlingit
light to our eyes
this morning, the day after Summer Solstice.

Endnotes

1. Jeremy Taylor, author of *The Wisdom of Your Dreams* and other books on dreamwork, email to poet, July 1, 2011.
2. Welsh Folk saying. Angelina is a donkey who resides at Lavender Dreams Farm and Donkey Rescue: www.lavenderdreamsfarm.com, www.facebook.com/DonkeyRescuer
3. R.I. Page, *Runes and Runic Inscriptions* (Suffolks: Boydell Press, 1995) p. 273; Ralph H. Blum, *The Book of Runes* (New York: St. Martin's Press, 2008) pp. 96-97; Susan Gray, *The Woman's Book of Runes* (New York: Barnes & Noble, 1999) pp. 26-30.
4. Nikolai Rimsky-Korsakov. "Flight of the Bumblebee," *The Tale of Tsar Saltan, Op. 57.;* John Kerry, quoted in "Syria chemical arms: 'Global red line' crossed – Kerry." *BBC News,* September 8, 2013. http://www.bbc.co.uk/news/world-europe-24008768
5. Ted Andrews, *Animal-Speak* (St. Paul: Llewellyn Publications, 1995) p. 134.
6. Andrews, *Animal-Speak,* p. 134.
7. Joe Coyhis, *Meditations with Native American Elders: The Four Seasons* (Coyhis Publishing & Consulting: Colorado Springs, 2007) p. 83.
8. Lewis Mehl-Madrone, *Healing the Mind Through the Power of Story* (Rochester: Bear and Company, 2010) p. 247.
9. Jude Siegel, *A Pacific Northwest Nature Sketchbook* (Portland: Timber Press, 2006), pp. 30-33.
10. Gray, *The Woman's Book of Runes,* p. 50.
11. Qur'an, 27:16 (The Noble Qu'ran).
12. Coyhis, *Meditations with Native American Elders,* p. 73.
13. Ray Legendre and Paul Suarez, "Police find two bodies in Washougal home," *The Columbian,* December 8, 2011.
14. Stephanie Austin, "Gemini Lunar Eclipse" *The Mountain Astrologer* 160, p. 103.
15. *Graces* – the three sister goddesses known in Greek mythology as Aglaia, Euphrosyne and Thalia who offer charm, wisdom and beauty.
16. Stephanie Austin, "Eco-Astrology Update," http://www.ecoastrology.com
17. Stuart Tomlinson, "Rescuer dives into Willamette River to save drowning man." *The Oregonian,* March 5, 2012.
18. Attributed as a Hopi saying
19. Miller, Andrea, "Path of Peace: The Life and Teachings of Sister Chan Khong," *Shambhala Sun,* May 2012, p. 39.
20. "SB Amtrak Train Kills Woman on Washington Tracks" *The Seattle Times,* June 27 2012.
21. Job. 12:7 (Author's Translation).

Acknowledgements

With gratitude to the editors of Hiraeth Press, Homebound Press and *Written River* as well as the following publications and organizations in which these poems, sometimes in slightly different form, have previously been honored or printed.

Crow Feathers, Red Ochre, Green Tea, Hiraeth Press: Color Wheel no. 2, Yellow Cedar (Ink and Dye on Paper)
Living Spiritually in a Consumer Society: Desire no. 2
Winged: New Writing on Bees (blog): Butternut Squash Soup
Written River: Autumn Equniox, Corvidae Gratitude, Deer Has Full Tail, She Speaks for the Bees, Spring Equinox

With gratitude to my beloved Judy, our family and friends, colleagues and *compañeras* for their love and support. With honor to all the thousands of people living with cancer and autoimmune disorders linked to environmental toxins, and to the earth for holding our pain. *Namaste* to many artists, chaplains, dreamers, holistic practitioners, musicians and writers who have provided critique, encouragement and inspiration. Gratitude to Karen Wood, Dawn Thompson, Sonali Balajee, Patricia Pearce, Kip Leitner, Peter Boehlke and Victoria Stein for holding a vision of creativity over the years. Gratitude to Erica Rayner-Horn for offering *Into the Depths of Winter Retreat* at her farm house in Maxwelton Valley. With thankfulness for writing residencies at Artsmith, Caldera and Soapstone. Gatherings and retreats at Commonweal, Ghost Ranch, Harmony Hill, Hollyhock, Sound Mind Center and Sitka Center for Art and Ecology have provided sacred space for renewal and writing. Special thanks to Michael Lerner, Francis Weller, Arlene Allsman, Kate Holcombe, Jnani Chapman and all of Commonweal and CCHP staff and volunteers. Much gratitude to Joan Borysenko, Sandra Ingerman, Mariana Romo-Carmona, Kim Stafford, Chase Twichell and writers who who have provided support to me and many poets and writers. Thanks to Stephanie Austin for gifting us with wisdom of astrologic insights every lunar cycle. Many blessings to Marci and David Van Ausdall, Angelina, Magic Sam and all the kindred spirits of Lavender Dreams Farm and Donkey Rescue. Many thanks to Susan Bourdet for her beautiful watercolor of "Snow Queen" on the book cover. *Namaste* to Jason Kirkey and Leslie M. Browning of Hiraeth Press and Homebound Press. This book emerged with the care of our larger community as well as the support of all our ancestors, angels, helping spirits and guides.

Mitakuye Oyasin – "We are all related."

About the Author

GWENDOLYN MORGAN learned the names of birds and wildflowers and inherited paint brushes and boxes from her grandmothers. With an M.F.A. in Creative Writing from Goddard College, and an M.Div. from San Francisco Theological Seminary and the Graduate Theological Union, she has been a recipient of artist and writing residencies at Artsmith, Caldera, Into the Depths of Winter, and Soapstone. *Crow Feathers, Red Ochre, Green Tea,* her first book of poems, was a winner of the Wild Earth Poetry Prize, Hiraeth Press. She has been published in numerous anthologies, blogs and literary journals. Gwendolyn and Judy A. Rose, her spouse, share their home with Abbey Skye, a rescued Pembroke Welsh Corgi.

ᚻIRAETH PRESS

¶ Poetry is the language of the earth. This
includes not only poems but the slow flap of
a heron's wings across the sky, the lightning of
its beak hunting in the shallow water; autumn
leaves and the smooth course of water over
stones and gravel. These, as much as poems,
communicate the being and meaning of things.
We strive to produce works of poetry, whether
they are actual poems or nonfiction. We are
passionate about poetry as a means of returning
the human voice to the chorus of the wild.

www.hiraethpress.com

CPSIA information can be obtained at www.ICGtesting.com
Printed in the USA
BVOW08s2022150916

462287BV00002B/2/P